Project title:
Fostering Sustainable Consumer Behaviour with Inclusive Bicycle Logistics Infrastructure in Urban Outskirts

Published by **Salzburg Research Forschungsgesellschaft m.b.H.**

Publish: BoD · Books on Demand GmbH, Überseering 33, 22297 Hamburg, bod@bod.de
Print: Libri Plureos GmbH, Friedensallee 273, 22763 Hamburg
ISBN: 978-3-8192-4858-0

This guidebook was written within the SuCoLo project: *https://sucolo.eu/*
By the following authors:

Michael Thelen (Salzburg Research)
Alexander Planitzer (VIABIRDS Technologies GmbH)
Dorina Tosaki (Salzburg Research)

This project has been funded by the Austrian Federal Ministry of Climate Action, Environment, Energy, Mobility, Innovation and Technology under the Driving Urban Transitions Partnership, which has been co-funded by the European Union under grant agreement no. 905465.

Table of Contents

1

About the guidebook

About the guidebook

Why sustainable logistics in (peri-)urban areas matter

To meet customers' growing demand for online shopping, without any adjustment, the top 100 cities globally will experience the following by 2030:

+36%
Delivery vehicles

+21%
Traffic congestion

+32%
Emissions

(World Economic Forum, 2020)

In the logistics process...

Adapted from Bell (n.d.)

First mile	Middle mile	Last mile

Manufacturer/ origin

Long distance transport

Inland transport

Warehouse & fulfillment

Delivery

Customer

...Up to 1/2 of total delivery CO2 emissions are from the last-mile segment
(Higgs et al., 2022)

As **urbanization continues to rise**, the demand for goods and services in peri-urban and urban areas has led to **increased transportation and logistics activities**. However, these areas are facing significant challenges related to the environmental and social impacts of logistics systems. High levels of **traffic congestion, air pollution, greenhouse gas emissions, and inefficient use of resources** are common consequences of traditional logistics practices.

In addition, the **growth of e-commerce** has further exacerbated these issues by **increasing the volume of deliveries and returns**, placing additional strain on urban infrastructure. **Sustainable logistics**, which aims to reduce the negative impact of transportation on both the environment and society, is essential to mitigating these challenges. To address these growing concerns, there is a pressing need for innovative solutions that promote greener, more efficient logistics systems in peri-urban and urban areas, ensuring **better quality of life** for residents and reducing the ecological footprint of urban logistics. This can take the forms of the use of **(e-)cargo bikes**, **parcel lockers, pick-up stations**, and **micro-hubs**.

What is this guidebook about?

Local policy-makers and regulators (e.g., city representatives) and logistics providers are faced with the challenge of promoting sustainable logistics in order to reduce CO_2 emissions, improve air quality, reduce noise, alleviate traffic congestion and make suburban and urban areas more livable. However, the use of **supply-side measures** (e.g., the procurement of clean delivery vehicles) **must be accompanied by aligned demand-side measures** to **promote**, **encourage** and **incentivise consumers to choose these options when it is offered to them**. In the context of online shopping, such demand-side measures can take the form of **digital nudges** to subtly guide shoppers to choose the sustainbable delivery option (which operate without restrictions or bans). A certain level of infrastructure (e.g., cargo bikes, pick-up stations and parcel lockers) need to be there for people to use it, however, understanding and fostering personal capabilities and motivations of people is also paramount.

The purpose of this guidebook is to provide a comprehensive, actionable approach to designing digital interventions that promote sustainable consumer delivery choices. Drawing on the latest behavioral science models, such as the COM-B Model (Michie et al., 2011), and offering step-by-step guidance on applying digital nudging, this guidebook aims to empower you to craft effective behavior change campaigns. By applying the insights and tools within, the guidebook seeks to support the creation of more sustainable, efficient, and consumer-friendly logistics system.

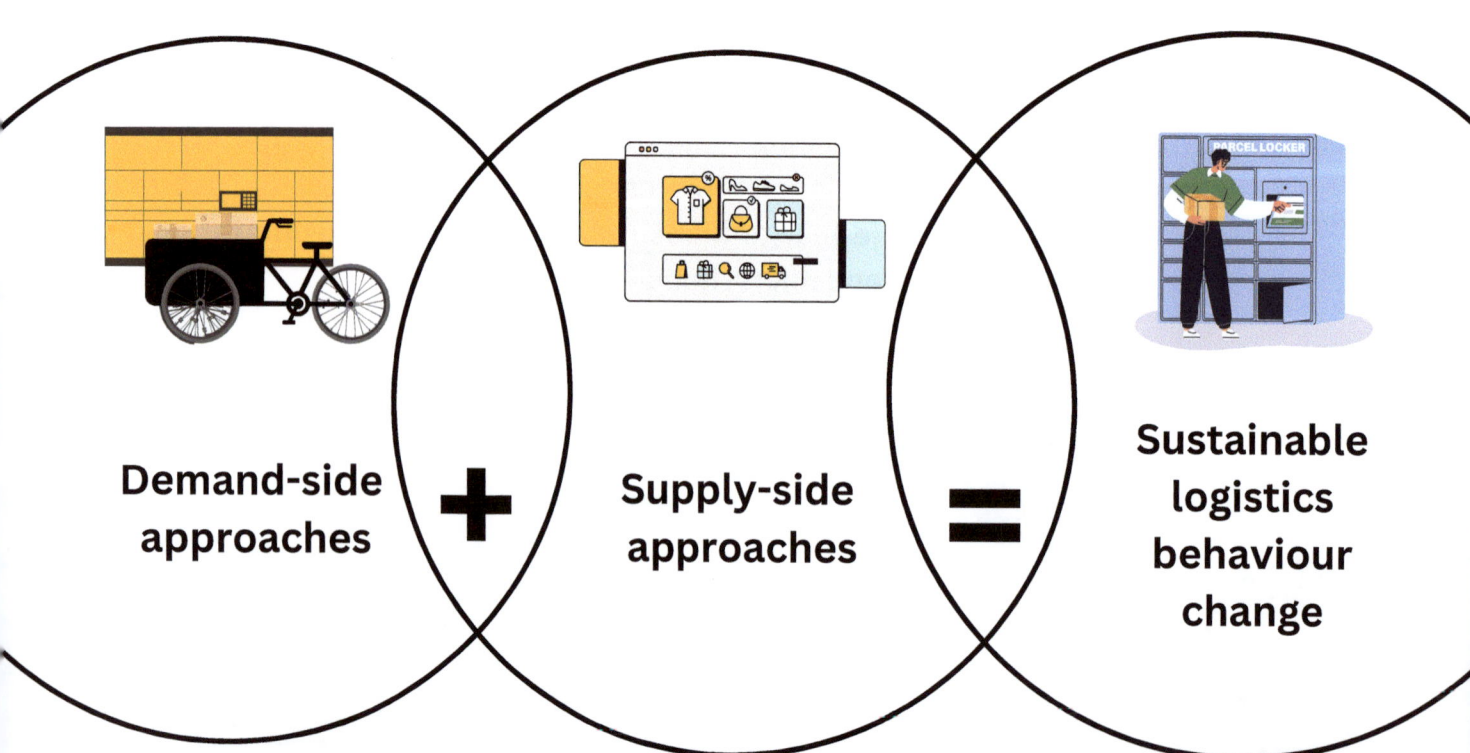

Demand-side approaches **+** **Supply-side approaches** **=** **Sustainable logistics behaviour change**

How will this guidebook benefit me?

◇ You will be equipped with practical, easy-to-apply strategies for influencing sustainable consumer behavior through nudges.

◇ You will understand the key behavioral drivers behind consumer decisions in the context of urban logistics.

◇ It offers proven methodologies, grounded in behavioral science, to design effective interventions for sustainability.

◇ The guidebook gives the tools to engage stakeholders & create tailored solutions for promoting sustainable logistics choices.

Who is this guidebook for?

E-commerce Businesses & Online Retailers
looking to encourage sustainable delivery choices among their customers through digital nudging

UX/UI Designers & Digital Product Teams
designing online shopping experiences and integrating behavioral nudges into user interfaces

Sustainability & Corporate Social Responsibility (CSR) Managers
working on reducing the environmental impact of e-commerce logistics and promoting sustainable consumer behavior

Marketing & Growth Teams
interested in leveraging behavioral insights to influence customer choices towards eco-friendly delivery options

Academics & Researchers
who could use the guidebook as a reference for further studies or practical applications

Policymakers & Regulators
focused on encouraging greener logistics through legislation and industry guidelines

2

A beginner's guide to behaviour change

What are the reasons behind people's behaviour?

Understanding why people behave the way they do can be explained through the **COM-B model**, which stands for one's capability, opportunity, and motivation (Michie et al., 2011). According to this model, behavior is shaped by the interaction of these three factors. **"C"**, or capability, refers to an individual's skills, knowledge, and physical ability to perform a behavior. For example, a person may need to understand how to choose a sustainable delivery option. **"O"**, or opportunity, involves the external factors that enable or limit behavior, like providing sustainable delivery choices in the first place. If eco-friendly delivery options are not offered or are inconvenient, people cannot choose them. Finally, **"M"**, or motivation, is the internal drive that influences decisions, including personal goals, emotions, and social influences. People may be more motivated to select sustainable options if they are aware of the positive impact or if others around them are making similar choices, for example. In short, the model demonstrates that a particular behaviour happens when one has the capability and opportunity to engage in it and is more motivated to engage in the said behaviour versus an alternative behaviour. The COM-B model helps us understand that **behavior change can be encouraged by addressing one or more of these factors, whether by improving capability, increasing opportunities, or boosting motivation.**

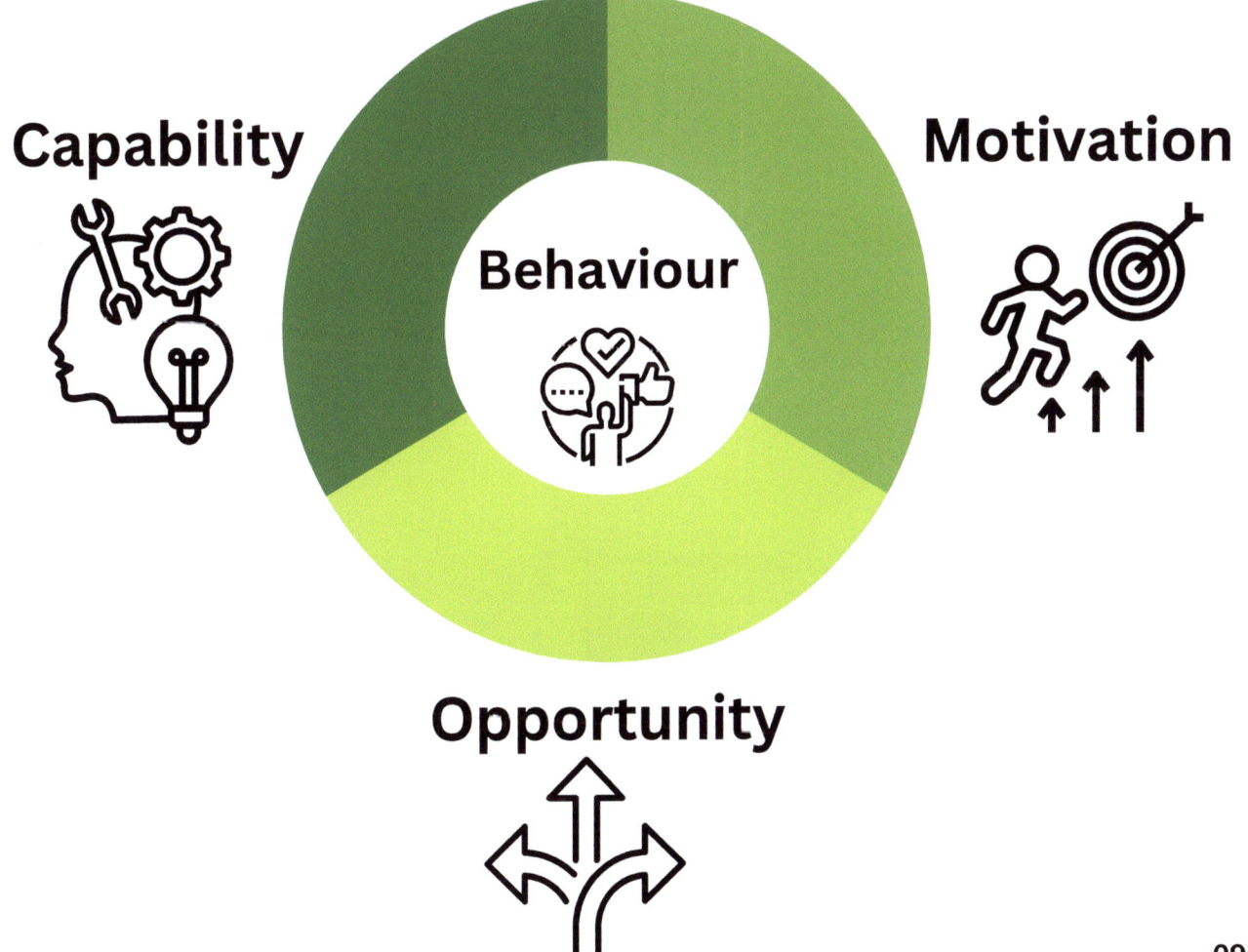

Capability

Motivation

Behaviour

Opportunity

3

Fostering behaviour change via digital nudging

Behavioural design & nudging

Behavioral interventions are methods used to steer people's decisions in a particular direction. One widely recognized approach is **nudging**, a concept introduced by Thaler and Sunstein in 2008. Unlike coercive methods that impose restrictions or financial penalties, nudging **maintains individual freedom of choice**. Instead, it subtly influences decision-making by **adjusting how options are presented within a given environment** — often referred to as choice architecture. This can involve reframing information, introducing new insights, or leveraging social feedback to encourage certain behaviors.

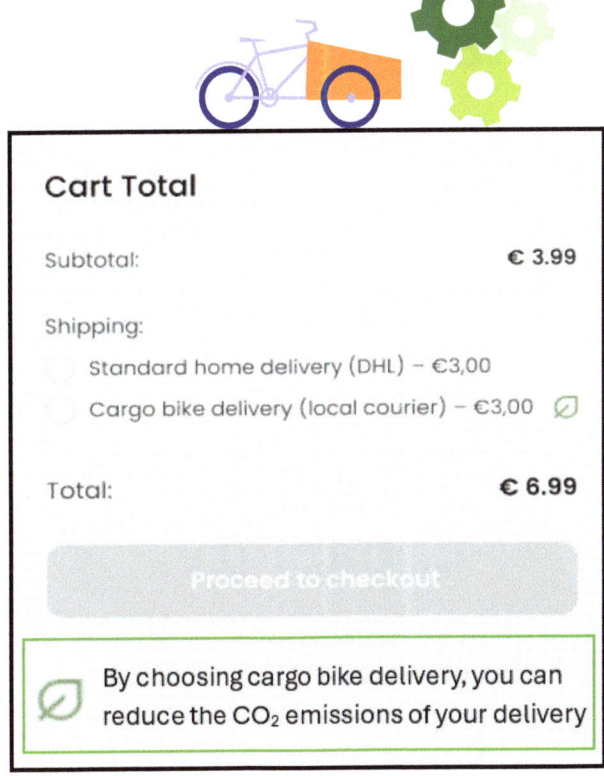

Throughout this handbook, we will frequently use the term nudging when discussing behavioral interventions, as it is a well-known and widely understood concept, particularly among policymakers and enterprises. In the following, we have listed examples of behavioural interventions for sustainable consumer delivery choices. As stated in the previous section, you might notice that the interventions target different aspects: some aim to increase one's motivation, some would like to improve individual capability and some want to create opportunities within the environment. In this way, **behavioural interventions are the methods to get rid of said obstacles that hinder a desired behaviour**. Here, you can design your own behavioural interventions for sustainable consumer delivery choices.

Example of nudging

If you have stayed in a hotel, perhaps you might have seen a sign next to the towels with a gentle reminder to reuse your towel when possible. This subtle placard serves to have you consider reusing your towel before reaching for another clean one.
Further reading: *https://www.green-nudges.com/*

Examples of behavioural interventions for sustainable consumer delivery choices

Target opportunity

Offer sustainable delivery options, such as cargo bikes or electric vehicles

Offer sustainable pick-up options, like at parcel lockers or pick-up stations

Target capability

Inform the customer of the environmental or social impacts of their delivery

Prompt or cue the customer of a broader issue related to sustainable delivery

Target motivation

Offer vouchers or extra customer loyalty points for choosing sustainable delivery

Foster a sense of urgency or scarcity of the sustainable delivery option

Closing the "green gap"

One's reported sustainability values and actual actions are often inconsistent. Even though customers may say certain sustainable attributes are important to them, this does not necessarily mean that they will always carry out behaviours that are in line with their values. This is why nudging must go beyond merely stating sustainability information and look at other elements in play that hinder them from choosing the desired option.

(ElHaffar et al., 2020)

Technology-Driven Behavior Change

In a review, Thelen et al. (2024) provided an overview of studies to date that tested the effectiveness of different nudges for sustainable consumer delivery choices on e-commerce sites. Such nudges also went beyond merely displaying sustainability information (e.g., amount of CO_2 saved), but also investigate how digital nudges that target other attributes have been explored in the literature. The top **five** most frequently employed digital nudge types in these studies are:

1 Information about social / environmental consequences

These nudges displayed sustainability labels (e.g., CO_2 calculation, a green leaf, number of trees saved) or highlighed social attributes (e.g., improved working conditions or increased safety)

 10g CO_2 saved

 16 trees saved

 Sustainable option

2 Social comparison

These nudges drew attention to others' performance to let them compare their behaviour as a benchmark by highlighting others' delivery choices

 70% of customers chose this delivery option

 This was chosen most often in the past month

3 Material incentive

Offering discounts and vouchers when the customer chooses the sustainable delivery option

 Get 5 extra loyalty points for this delivery

 Receive a 2 euro discount for this delivery

4   *Digital default*

Setting the sustainable delivery option as the pre-chosen, default option

5   *Social media sharing*

Letting the customer know that their choice of the sustainable delivery option is exemplary, and offering them the option to share their delivery selection on their social media page

(Classifications of behaviour change techniques according to Michie et al., 2013)

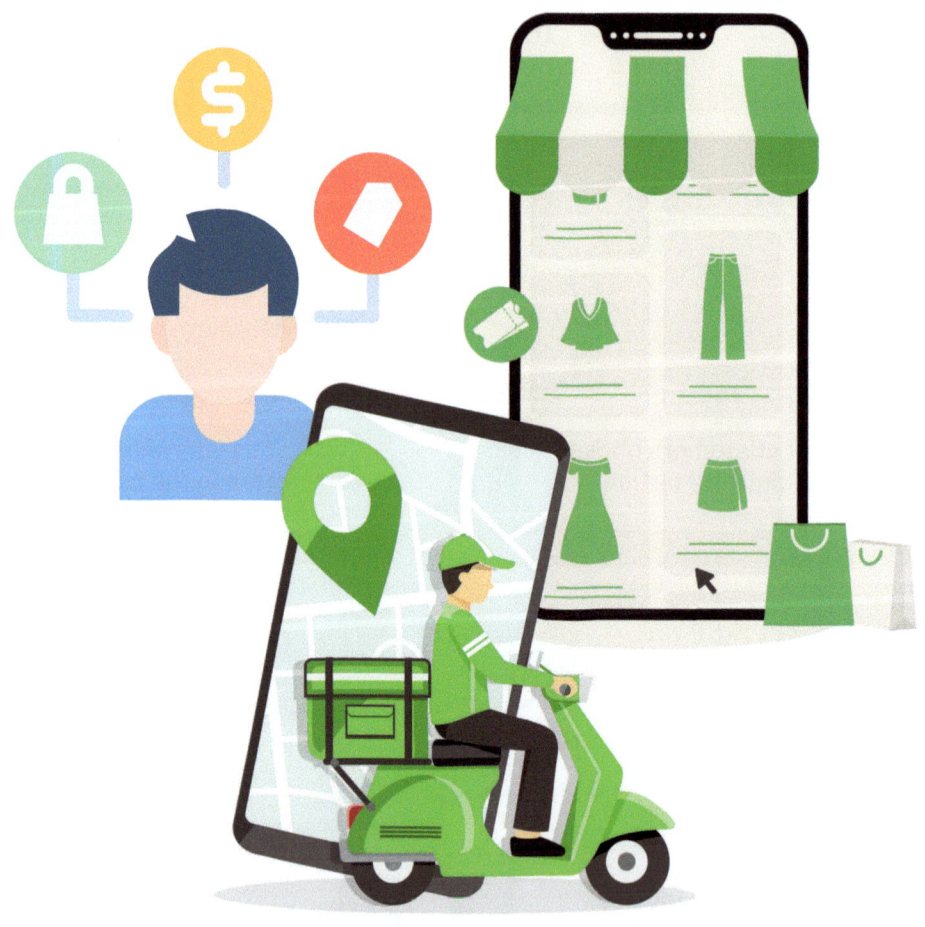

Crafting your own digital nudges

Now that we have had an introduction, digital nudging and its applications to encourage sustainable consumer delivery, you can get started with crafting your own digital nudges. In doing so, we recommend that you take several steps to think about the best course of action for your specific case.

Outline the problem that you would like to overcome

Define your desired behavioural outcome & target group

Determine the barriers that hinder the behaviour

Define behaviour change activities to remove the barrier(s)

(According to Rubinstein, 2018)

1 **Outline the problem that you would like to overcome**

First of all, it is important to nail down the exact problem in your specific case that you would like to alleviate with the use of digital nudging. Perhaps there is too much CO_2 in your neighboorhood, or perhaps your neighborhood is experiencing too much traffic congestion (for example, from 8am to 10am). Or, perhaps the problem is that not enough shops in your locality offer sustainable delivery options, or that the local post is overburdened with a high volume of return parcels. Here, it is imperative that your problem definition is as detailed as possible. For city planners, there is not a one-size-fits-all solution and needs to be contextualized.

Below are some examples of problems that one might experience:

The sharp increase in e-commerce has led to more delivery vehicles, raising CO_2 emissions and worsening air quality in urban areas.

The high volume of e-commerce returns is causing additional traffic and inefficient routing, increasing congestion and emissions.

Delivery vans double-parking and idling on busy streets create bottlenecks, slowing down public transport and increasing safety risks for pedestrians and cyclists.

The absence of strategically located micro-fulfillment centers forces long delivery routes, reducing efficiency and increasing traffic.

The rising volume of parcel deliveries is exceeding the capacity of existing infrastructure, leading to frequent delays, increased traffic, and inefficient use of city space.

While many local online shops are open to using green delivery, they struggle to promote these options effectively that goes beyond offering discounts or incentives.

2 ▸ Define your desired behavioural outcome & target group

Specifying this as precisely as possible will help in the next steps where we think about barriers for alternative behaviour. As well, who are you trying to reach? Online shoppers have diverse characteristics, and zeroing on these aspects as much as possible is a success factor for creating targeted nugdes that attract this audience. For example, a desired behavioural outcome could be:

Online shoppers aged 18 and over living in Austria who shop online at least two times per year should choose the cargo bike delivery option when it is offered to them.

 **Determine the barriers that hinder the behaviour**

You can begin by identifying all the reasons why this target group is engaging in a different behavior instead of the desired one. Gather insights by speaking with your target audience or analyzing existing data. For an initial assessment, consider the barriers in terms of **motivation** or **capability**, as we assume that a sustainable delivery method (i.e., the opportunity) is available. Here are some examples:

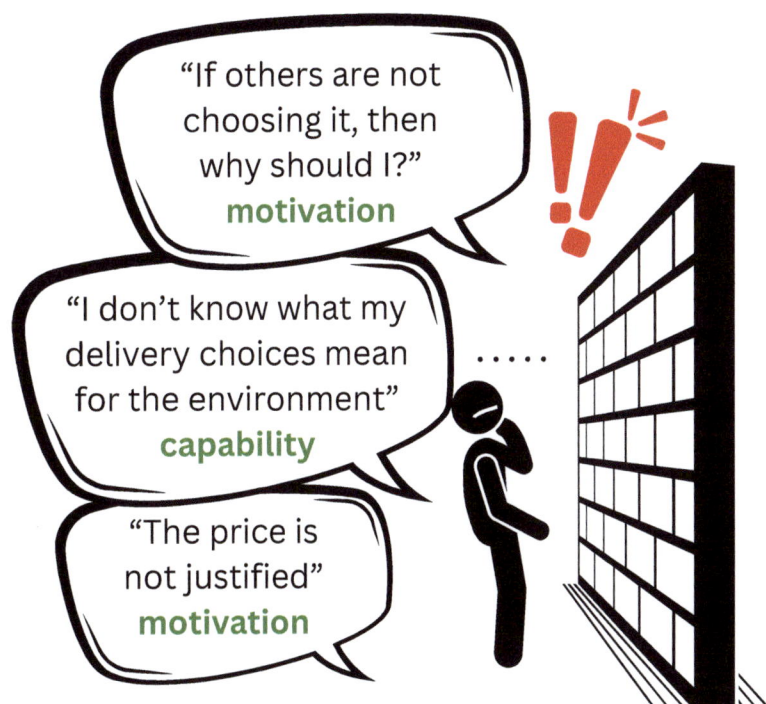

 **Define behaviour change activities to remove the barrier(s)**

In the case of developing digital nudges to get online shoppers to choose sustainable modes of delivery, we believe that *education*, *incentivisation*, *persuasion* and *enviromental restructuring* are the ideal behaviour change activities to address the most prominent barriers.

<u>Activity type</u>	<u>Addresses</u>
 **Education** Increasing knowledge or understanding	• Capability (psychological) • Motivation (reflective)
 **Incentivisation** Creating expectation of reward	• Motivation (reflective) • Motivation (automatic)
 **Persuasion** Inducing positive or negative feelings or stimulate action	• Motivation (reflective) • Motivation (automatic)
 **Environmental restructuring** Changing the physical or social context	• Motivation (automatic)

(According to Michie et al., 2011)

Soumaya

Age: 27, lives in St. Gallen, Switzerland
Occupation: Corporate lawyer
Shopping behaviour: Avid online shopper, shops often online
Current behaviour: Most of the time, opts for standard delivery
Barriers: Although she often shops sustainably, she does not know which delivery option is the most sustainable
Removing barriers with nudge: An educational nudge that informs her, out of all the listed delivery methods, which is the most sustainable with a green leaf icon

Jamal

Age: 47, lives in Utrecht, the Netherlands
Occupation: Car salesman
Shopping behaviour: Moderate online shopper, shops occassionally online
Current behaviour: Always opts for the cheapest delivery option
Barriers: He is not willing to spend that much extra for sustainable delivery
Removing barriers with nudge: An incentivising nudge notifying him that if he chooses the sustainable delivery option, he will receive a small discount on his next purchase

Examples of digital nudges for sustainable consumer delivery options

In this section, you will find examples of digital nudges that remove the barriers to opportunity, motivation and capability (as described in Michie et al., 2011), which can help you on your quest to design your own behavioural interventions.

Opportunities

Interventions for opportunity usually entail changing the environment a person is in. In the case of sustainable delivery, opportunity mainly refers to making sure that the consumers are afforded the chance to have such options available to them while they are shopping (e.g., cargo bike delivery, pick-up at a parcel locker or pick-up station).

Motivation

Motivation has a strong individual flavour and might take a different form depending on the person. Understanding the distinction between **automatic and reflective motivation** is crucial for designing effective behavior change interventions, as it helps identify whether behaviors are driven by automatic impulses or thoughtful deliberation. Automatic motivation involves unconscious processes such as one's desires and impulses that drive behavior without deliberate thought. These are the instinctive reactions and emotional responses that can prompt immediate actions. Reflective motivation, on the other hand, entails conscious processes like evaluations, plans, and intentions. This form of motivation involves deliberate decision-making, where individuals consider the pros and cons before engaging in a behavior.

Below are some examples of how to target somebody's automatic and reflective motivation:

Automatic motivation

- *In the order of delivery options, display the sustainable one first*
- *Pre-select the sustainable delivery as the default*

Reflective motivation

- Offer a voucher or extra loyalty points if sustainable delivery is chosen
- Inform that other shoppers are choosing sustainable delivery

Capabilities

Capabilities can be both psychological or physical. In the context of online shopping, psychological capabilities (e.g., one's knowledge, skills and attention) especially are an important component due to the cognitive nature of online shopping.

Below are some examples of how to target psychological capability:

Psychological capability

- Inform which delivery option is the most sustainable
- Inform of the delivery choices' environmental or social consequences

 Here, physical capabilities (e.g., physical abilities, fitness levels) are of secondary importance; however, a basic threshold must be met. Those with a disability (e.g., seeing impairments) pose a challange in this context. Having said that, the digital nudges described in this guidebook cannot necessarily be catered to this group.

Finding the right digital nudges for your case

Now, with different digital nudges in mind, it is time to choose which nudges you will implement. For this purpose, the different nudges can be ranked upon certain attributes that you find important. Here, we recommend utilising the APEASE criteria from West et al. (2019), which ranks behavioural interventions according to their level of **acceptability**, **practicability**, **effectiveness**, **affordability**, **side-effects** and **equity**. After ranking each nudge based of these six criteria on a scale from zero to ten, you can reflect upon the highest ranked ideas. (A template is included in the Section *Canvases and Inspiration*)

The components of the APEASE criteria

Acceptability
How far is it acceptable to key stakeholders? This includes the target group, potential funders, practitioners delivering the interventions and relevant community and commercial groups.

Practicability
Can it be implemented at scale within the intended context, material and human resources? What would need to be done to ensure that the resources and personnel were in place, and is the intervention sustainable?

Effectiveness
How effective is the intervention in achieving the policy objective(s)? How far will it reach the intended target group and how large an effect will it have on those who are reached?

Affordability
How far can it be afforded when delivered at the scale intended? Can the necessary budget be found for it? Will it provide a good return on investment?

Side-effects
What are the chances that it will lead to unintended adverse or beneficial outcomes?

Equity
How far will it increase or decrease differences between advantaged and disadvantaged sectors of society?

(West at al., 2019)

Practical integration on a webshop

Integrating digital nudges to promote green delivery choices on a webshop can be technically simple or more involved, depending on the complexity and personalization of the nudge. Basic nudges—such as highlighting the greenest delivery option, reordering choices to set eco-friendly options as the default, or using encouraging wording—can often be implemented directly via the webshop's content management system (CMS) or front-end code (HTML/CSS). In many cases, no additional plug-in is needed; it's more about thoughtful placement and design decisions that align with behavioral insights.

For more advanced nudging strategies, such as personalized recommendations based on past behavior, dynamic incentives, or real-time calculations of environmental impact (also known as algorithmic nudging), deeper technical integration is required. These types of nudges typically need access to customer data, shipping information, and possibly external application programming interfaces (APIs) to calculate emissions or delivery footprints. In such cases, custom plug-ins or server-side scripts may be necessary to handle the logic and data processing. Integration with existing webshop platforms (like Shopify, WooCommerce, or Magento) should consider compatibility, data privacy regulations (e.g., GDPR), and the ability to update nudge logic as needed.

Overall, the integration effort scales with the complexity of the nudge. Simple nudges are low-cost and easy to implement, while more personalized or dynamic ones require coordination between UX designers, developers, and sometimes even data scientists. Whichever the case, a clear plan and understanding of the technical environment can help ensure smooth implementation and measurable impact.

4
Things to keep in mind

Navigating digital nudges: Our recommendations

Taking into account our experience in designing digital nudges for sustainable consumer delivery choices, we propose that you keep the following **six recommendations** in mind:

 Mitigate cart abandonment

 Reduce cognitive overload

 Prioritise nudges that are easily implementable

 Discuss the nudge internally & externally

 Avoid misleading sustainability claims

 Keep data protection at the forefront

Mitigate cart abandonment

It is important to incorporate digital nudges that do not come at the expense of online shoppers abandoning their carts last minute due to too much information, confusion or disinterest.

Neutrality
Make sure the nudge does not invoke negative feelings among the shopper.

Subtlety
Avoid employing nudges that are too intrusive, such as extensive pop-ups.

 # Reduce cognitive overload

Building upon the first point, an important aspect of mitigating cart abandonment is to reduce cognitive overload.

Ease
Take steps to mitigate unnecessary stimuli by employing seamless, simple and easy-to-understand nudges.

Simplicity
Avoid the use of too many graphics and long text that can overwhelm the user.

 # Prioritise nudges that are easily implementable

Many online shops do not have the resources to integrate intricate, complex nudges on their website (such as algorithmic nudging). The good news is that this is not at all necessary - effective nudges can be created with a few simple edits.

Less is more
Start out with simple nudges, such as displaying a green leaf. Over time, you can always work your way up towards experimenting with more elaborate ones!

Discuss the nudge internally & externally

To avoid personal bias, it is best to discuss which nudges you would like to implement with your team to make sure it complements your overall business strategy and goals. Additionally, if you have the means, it is a good idea to explore the nudges with a group of external stakeholders, e.g., other fellow online shoppers.

Teamwork — Ensure that whichever nudge you choose is consensually agreed upon with your team.

Inclusivity — Leverage the perspectives of outside stakeholders (i.e., "the crowd") to add feedback and help co-design the most optimal nudges for your case.

Avoid misleading sustainability claims

As important as it is to promote sustainable aspects of delivery options as much as possible, it is paramount to promote only information that is factual and can be backed up. In fact, there is even legislation developed to combat so-called "greenwashing".

Compliance — Ensure that your nudges can be substantiated and is in line with legislation, such as the EU Proposal for a Green Claims Directive (Directive 2023/0085). However, inform yourself of the proper legislation that is applicable for your own context!

Keep data protection at the forefront

Regardless of which nudges you decide to employ, it is critical that user data of affected parties follows applicable data protection legislation, such as the General data Protection Regulation (GDPR) (Regulation 2016/679).

Privacy — Whether or not your nudges will incorporate user data, it is a best practice to verify that your e-commerce operations wholly adhere to data protection legislation.

5

Canvases & inspiration

It's time to get started to design digital nudges for sustainable consumer delivery choices!

Personas: Who are the target customers you wish to reach?

Name:
Age:
Location:
Occupation:
Shopping behaviour:

Current behaviour:

Barriers:

Removing barriers with nudge:

Name:
Age:
Location:
Occupation:
Shopping behaviour:

Current behaviour:

Barriers:

Removing barriers with nudge:

  Published by
salzburg**research**

Canvas: Defining target behaviour and barriers

Outline the problem that you would like to overcome

Define your desired behavioural outcome & target group

Determine the barriers that hinder the behaviour

Define behaviour change activities to remove the barrier(s)

Published by
salzburg**research**

Sustainable delivery campaigns in your locality: What do you face?

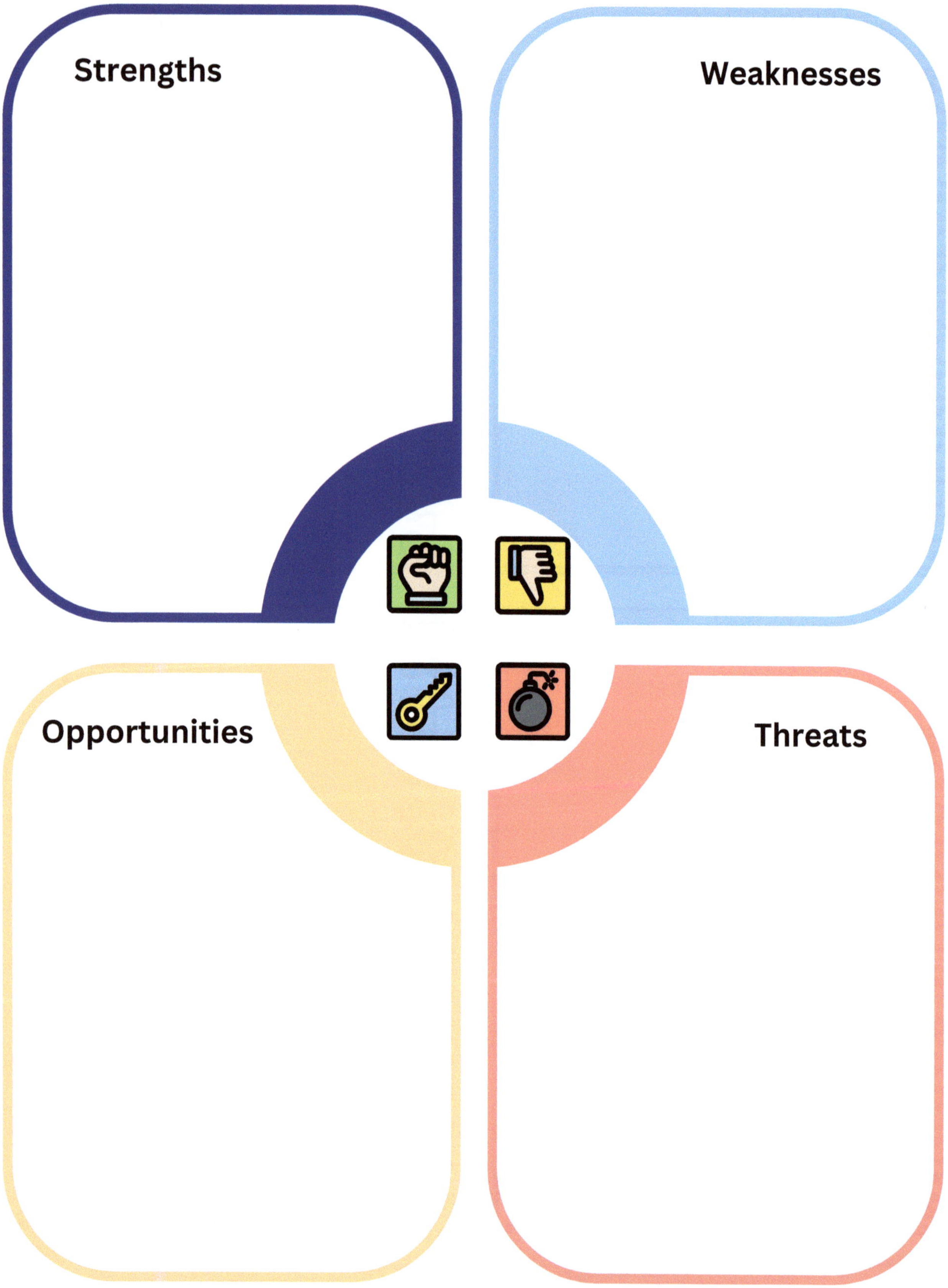

Strengths

Weaknesses

Opportunities

Threats

  **Published by** salzburg**research**

Which stakeholders are needed to realise your sustainable delivery nudging campaign?

Citizens

City officials

UX/UI designers

Data suppliers

Logistics providers

E-commerce sites

31

Published by
salzburg**research**

What would the ideal delivery nudge look like for you?

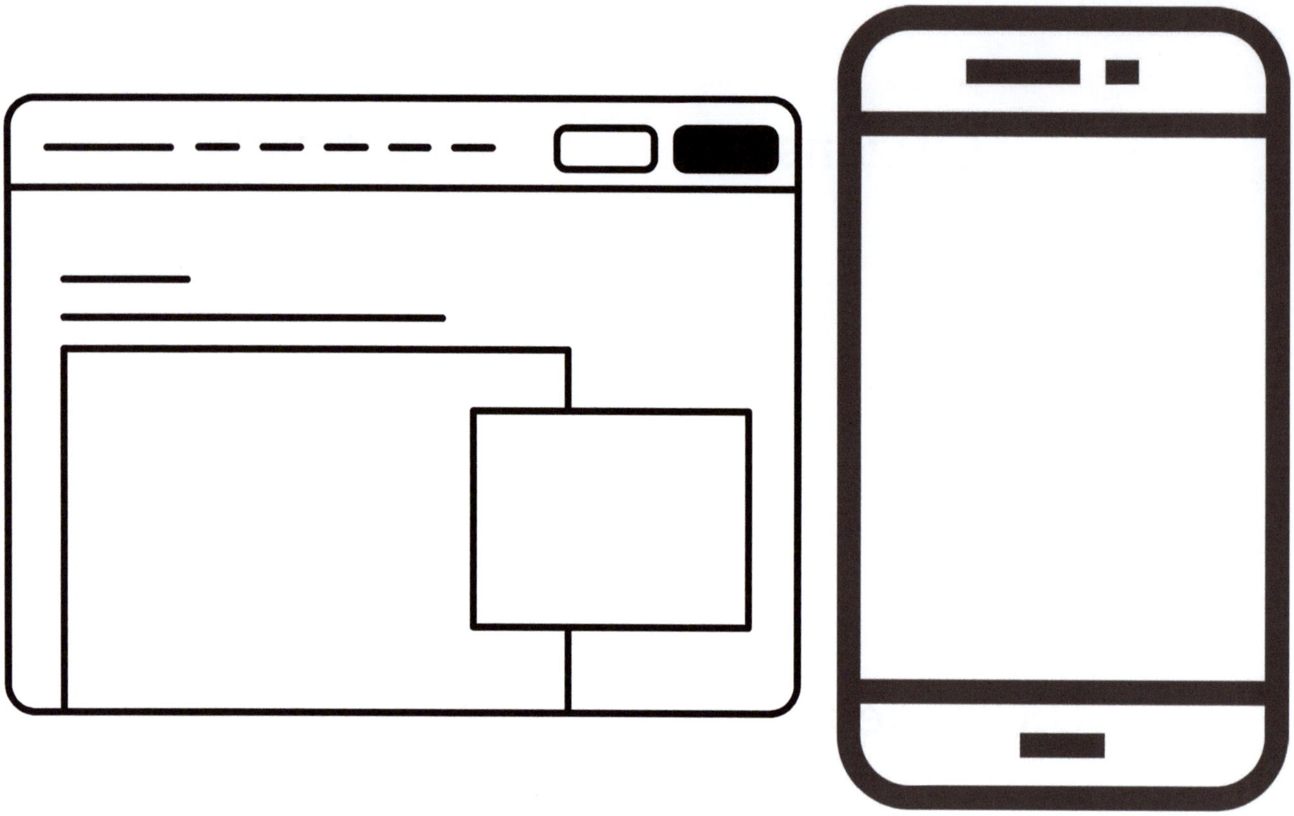

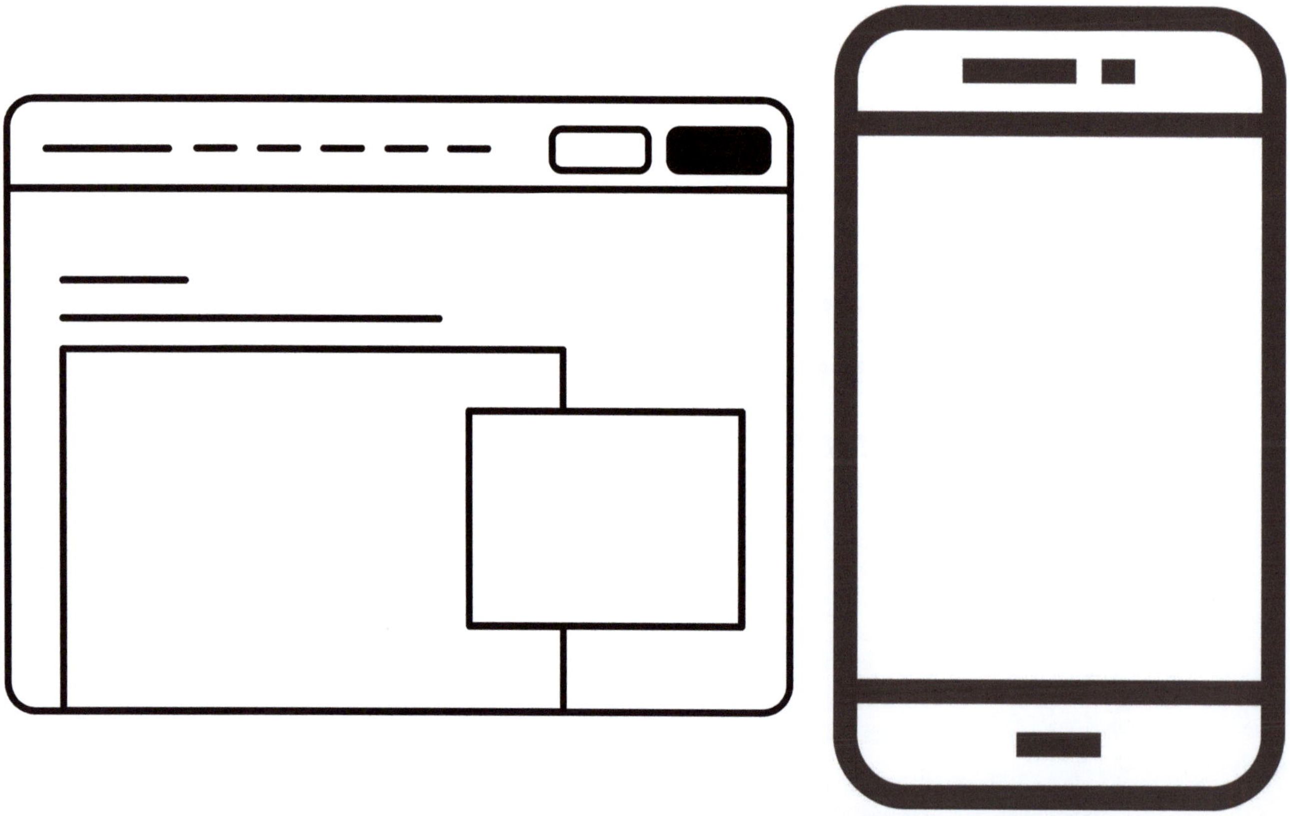

Published by
salzburg**research**

Ranking and prioritising your digital nudges using the APEASE criteria

Rate each component on a scale from zero to ten

Nudge	Acceptability	Practicability	Effectiveness	Affordability	Side-effects	Equity

(West at al., 2019)

6

References & further reading

1. Bell, R. (n.d.). Last Mile Delivery Explained: Trends, Challenges, Costs & More. Retrieved March 3, 2025, from *https://www.merchantsfleet.com/industry-insights/what-is-last-mile-delivery/*

2. Directive 2023/0085(COD). Proposal for Directive (EU) No 0085/2023 of the European Parliament and of the Council of 3 March 2023 on substantiation and communication of explicit environmental claims. *https://eur-lex.europa.eu/legal-content/EN/TXT/PDF/?uri=CELEX:52023PC0166*

3. ElHaffar, G., Durif, F., & Dubé, L. (2020). Towards closing the attitude-intention-behavior gap in green consumption: A narrative review of the literature and an overview of future research directions. Journal of Cleaner Production, 275, 122556. *https://doi.org/10.1016/j.jclepro.2020.122556*

4. Green Nudges. (n.d.). Retrieved March 3, 2025, from *https://www.green-nudges.com/*

5. Higgs, G., Katta, A., Lam, P., Tumer, A., Leistman, V., Krogh, M., Sreenivas, S., Gopal, S., Mann, H., & Robertson, A. (2022). Revealing the secret emissions of e-commerce. *https://clean-mobility.org/wp-content/uploads/2022/07/Secret-Emissions-of-E-Commerce.pdf*

6. Michie, S., Richardson, M., Johnston, M., Abraham, C., Francis, J., Hardeman, W., Eccles, M. P., Cane, J., & Wood, C. E. (2013). The behavior change technique taxonomy (v1) of 93 hierarchically clustered techniques: Building an international consensus for the reporting of behavior change interventions. Annals of Behavioral Medicine, 46(1), 81–95. *https://doi.org/10.1007/s12160-013-9486-6*

7. Michie, S., van Stralen, M. M., & West, R. (2011). The behaviour change wheel: A new method for characterising and designing behaviour change interventions. Implementation Science, 6(1). *https://doi.org/10.1186/1748-5908-6-42*

8. Regulation (EU) 2016/679 of the European Parliament and of the Council of 27 April 2016 on the protection of natural persons with regard to the processing of personal data and on the free movement of such data, and repealing Directive 95/46/EC (General Data Protection Regulation). *http://data.europa.eu/eli/reg/2016/679/oj*

9. Rubinstein, H. (2018). Applying Behavioural Science to the Private Sector: Decoding What People Say and What They Do. Palgrave Macmillan.

10. Thaler, R. H., & Sunstein, C. R. (2008). Nudge: Improving Decisions About Health, Wealth, and Happiness. Pengiun.

11. Thelen, M., Hornung-Praehauser, V., & Leistner, D. (2024). Exploring Digital Behaviour Interventions to encourage Sustainable Consumer Delivery Choices. 2024 NOFOMA Conference "Logistics and Supply Chain Management in a Risky and Uncertain World." *https://www.researchgate.net/publication/386905474_Exploring_Digital_Behaviour_Interventions_to_encourage_Sustainable_Consumer_Delivery_Choices*

12. West, R., Michie, S., Atkins, L., Chadwick, P., & Lorencatto, F. (2019). Achieving behaviour change: A guide for local government and partners. *https://assets.publishing.service.gov.uk/media/5e7b4e85d3bf7f133c923435/PHEBI_Achieving_Behaviour_Change_Local_Government.pdf*

13. World Economic Forum. (2020). The Future of the Last-Mile Ecosystem. *https://www.weforum.org/publications/the-future-of-the-last-mile-ecosystem/*